To Nanna and Pop, whose love and light continue to shine through our family.
To my boys, may you always approach the world with a sense of wonder and curiosity,
and may your inner light be your guide.
And to the thought leaders who continue to light the way forward, thank you for inspiring us
with your wisdom.

Little Light

Written by Amanda Rimkus
Illustrated by Mehrab Alif

Copyright © 2025 Amanda Rimkus

All rights reserved. No part of this book may be reproduced
in any manner whatsoever without prior written permission
of the publisher.

First Printing, 2025

Published by Sense of Wonder
www.senseofwonder.com.au

ISBN 978-1-7643653-0-7

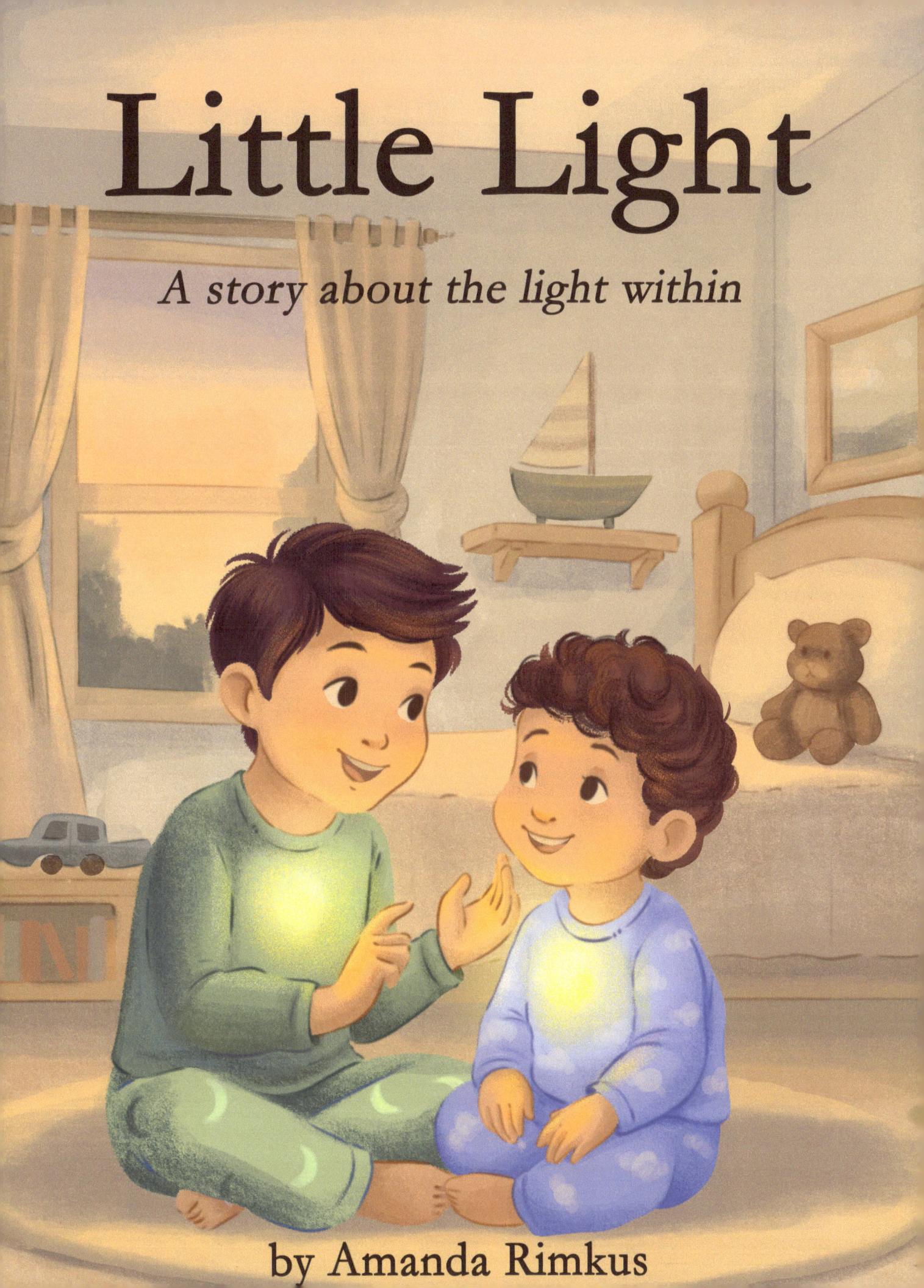

In a little town where dreams came to play, lived children with lights tucked safely away. Deep in their hearts, like lighthouses aglow, their lights showed them kindness wherever they'd go.

It was the night before Lucas's first day of school. Thoughts raced through his head. *Everything is going to be new,* he thought. *New classroom, new teacher, new friends.*

Butterflies fluttered in his belly. He was so nervous, his light began to flicker.
He went to his mum. "What if no one plays with me tomorrow? What if no one is nice? What if I don't make any friends?"

His mum smiled. "I'm sure you'll meet kind, caring, and thoughtful friends," she said. "They will make your light feel warm and bright. They will be your *cheerleader* friends."
Lucas sat up. "So everyone at school will be nice?"

"Well..." Mum started. "Not quite. Some might be *dimmer* friends. They may say hurtful things or act unkindly. And that's okay. They could be having a bad day. Or they might be just as nervous about the first day of school as you are."

She pulled Lucas into a hug. "Most importantly, only *you* will know which friends help your light shine. Just remember, shine bright, little light."

As Lucas stepped into his classroom on the first day, his heart thumped. He took a deep breath and remembered his mum's words: *Shine bright, little light.*

During art, Lucas sat next to Aisha. "I like your green caterpillar," she said. "Want to use my red flower sticker?"

Lucas smiled. His light glowed warm and bright. *Aisha is a kind friend*, he thought. *Shine bright, little light!*

At recess the next day, Noah saw Lucas sitting alone.
"Wanna build a sandcastle together?" he asked.
When their tower tumbled, Noah laughed and said, "Let's try again!"
Lucas felt safe and happy. *Noah helps my light shine too*, he thought.

After lunch, Mia said,
"I saw you climb all the way up the spider web! You're so brave!"
Lucas's cheeks turned pink, and his light began to sparkle.
Mia is a cheerleader friend, he thought. *She sees the good things in me. Shine bright, little light!*

Later that week, Lucas was colouring with James. "My favourite colour is green," James said. When Lucas shared that his was purple, James smiled. "Friends don't have to like the same things. We just have to like being together."

Lucas felt his light get even brighter. *Kind words like that make my light feel bright!* he thought. *Shine bright, little light!*

But not everyone helped Lucas's light shine. One afternoon, Finn pushed in front of him. "You're too slow," he snapped.
When Lucas tried to join a game on the playground, Finn shouted, "We don't need you!"

It wasn't the first time. That morning, Finn had said, "You're not my friend unless you do what I say!" Lucas's light flickered. It felt small and quiet. He thought, *Finn is acting like a dimmer friend today.*

Their teacher noticed and spoke to them. "Some days, our light may flicker. Maybe your day didn't start out right, or maybe your favourite toy broke. But even on those days, we can still choose to be kind."

She looked at Finn. "A dimmer friend is someone who puts out another person's light. The more light and kindness we share, the brighter our lights shine. Just remember, shine bright, little light."

That night, Lucas told Mum about Finn. "He was a dimmer friend today. My light felt small because he didn't let me play with everyone."

Mum gave him a hug. "Sometimes people do that because they're having a hard time too," she said. "That's when you start building your bubble of trust."

"What's that?" Lucas asked.

"It's made of people who help your light shine bright again and again. They are kind and cheer you on. Have you met any cheerleader friends at school yet?"

Lucas nodded. "I think Aisha, Noah, Mia, and James help my light shine."

"Good!" Mum said. "And have you helped anyone else's light shine?"

Lucas nodded. "Today, James threw a stick that bumped into me. He felt really bad, and I said, 'It's okay, James. I know it was an accident.'"

Mum smiled. "When we are kind and gentle, we help each other's light shine even brighter."

The next day, Lucas noticed Finn sitting alone, frowning at his lunchbox.
Lucas took a deep breath and walked over.
"Hey Finn, want to play with us after lunch?"

Finn looked up, surprised. Slowly, a small smile appeared. "Yeah... okay," he said quietly.

As they played, Finn laughed for the first time that day. Something warm flickered inside him. His light was starting to shine.

Lucas smiled to himself. *Shine bright, little light.*

At bedtime, Lucas told his mum about playing with Finn. "Kindness can turn even the dimmest lights bright again," she said. Then she tucked him in and whispered, "Can you feel it? Your light is always there. It's okay if it dims sometimes. Only you know how to make it bright again."

Lucas closed his eyes. He had found his superpower: knowing when his light was shining, and how to help it glow.

Message to Grown-Ups

This story helps children navigate their feelings, recognise healthy and unhealthy interactions, understand boundaries, and build emotional awareness while gently introducing the idea of personal sovereignty through the metaphor of an 'inner light.'
It also supports children in learning to honour their inner light, trust their sense of self, and make choices that protect their wellbeing.

You can extend the story by inviting children to reflect on questions such as:
- Did anyone make your light shine bright today? How did that feel?
- Who are your kind, safe, cheerleader friends?
- Did someone act like a "dimmer" friend today? How did that make you feel?
- What helps you feel better when your light feels dim?

You might also like to share some of your own stories or moments when your light shone brightly, places that filled you with joy, or times when someone was a cheerleader friend to you. Sharing your own experiences helps children feel supported, understood, and deeply connected.

www.ingramcontent.com/pod-product-compliance
Lightning Source LLC
Chambersburg PA
CBHW041508220426

43661CB00017B/1280